A Work of Poetry
Past, Present, and Future

John Williamson

VANTAGE PRESS
New York

Cover design by Susan Thomas

FIRST EDITION

Published by Vantage Press, Inc.
419 Park Ave. South, New York, NY 10016

Manufactured in the United States of America
ISBN: 978-0-533-15657-3

Library of Congress Catalog Card No.: 2006909092

0 9 8 7 6 5 4 3 2 1

Contents

The Effect That Comes with Time

After carefully giving some thought to
How time relentless passes away
And the many things it robs us of
As it silently goes on its way

First it takes away childhood
And most of its memories as well
Waiting for us to become youths
To take from us precious years as well

As we arrive at what is called adulthood
The coming of age I do believe
Time's relentless pursuit has not eased
From its activity, no one is relieved

As its silent march goes forth
Its toll being left in its wake
Not easily seen or understood
The subtle changes that life do take

Not only do it rob us of our youth
And make us old in every way
Our physical and mental health it take
Leaving us with pain day to day

From here on life is downhill
Time's pursuit has made its mark
All things it has robbed us of
Are lost as if forever in the dark

God's Master Worker

The creative work of God is
Work of long ago
That are so enduring remaining
Even to this day
Attesting to His perfection
In wisdom they aglow
Honoring Him with due respect
Alluding to His way

He had a master worker
In days of long ago
He instructed him in all things
And taught him aright
Preparing him for the glory
On him He would bestow
Who abounded in joy in knowledge
He found wisdom and delight

This master worker had a share in
God's creative plan
Another role he would fulfill his
Coming here to earth
After him all other things were
Placed in his hands
He gave up his heavenly origin for a
Miraculous coming birth

When he was here he came to be known
As earth's greatest man
The work he did when he was here
There could be no compare
The record show the things he did
With us yet remain
That all might know and can never say
Of this I am unaware

Leave Presumption Alone

When something has been said
or done
Bring forth a woeful cry
When unplanned action
And hastiness of words
Cause an unkind reply

To act presumptuous and give
no thought
To and how others might feel
Then try to justify the wrong
By saying it is no big deal

Hurtful deeds and unkind
Words
Bring scars that are hard to heal
Imprinted in the heart and mind
Are ever being revealed

Being presumptuous go hand
In hand
With arrogance of heart
Failing to heed outspoken words
Of the mouth before they depart

So be careful of what you do
Or say
And leave presumption alone
The feeling of those that you hurt
You might never be able to atone

Dedicated to Time

I have often said I need more time
The allotted time is not enough time
To work within this frame of time
To do what is required at this time

Some time is better than no time
When that is required call for time
To accomplish something on time
Cannot be called lost time

Lost time is past time of time
Time lost in the stream of time
Cannot be recalled from past time
So it is called wasted time

Wasted time is time of present time
Time that will soon be past time
Can't be made up with future time
Now it has become wasted time

The father of time is slow time
Who travels with the flow of time
Fleeting time which is fast time
Help him to arrive on time

We should make good our present time
Before it becomes our past time
By preparing now for a future time
We might inherit everlasting time

The Rage of the Storm

I lifted my eyes toward the sky
To watch the clouds go drifting by
All size and shape they did form
Covering the sky for the coming storm

Ashen in color they did appear
Growing darker as they drifted near
On the current of the wind they ride
As waves of the sea on its rolling tide

Horizon to horizon they cover the sky
On a mission they knew why
Waiting to give birth from on high
The rain it has held way up high

First the calm as the wind grow still
The smell of rain the earth is filled
The thunder boom the downpour come
The wind in an uproar the hail come

The sky is ashen the downpour is immense
The wind aroused adds to the suspense
The lightning cracks the thunder boom
As uncertain on the horizon loom

The storm vents its rage then moves on
A lull sets in after the storm is gone
The sky again become crystal clear
All things again reside not in fear

The storm come without much concern
The rage of its fury should be discern
The havoc of its power can't be blamed
On the one who can the storm tame

Holy Spirit

God's holy spirit has been moving
From days of long ago
Working to do His will
That He foretold long ago

From an eon of time and onward
It is doing what He desire to do
Fulfilling all of His purposes
For making all things new

The wondrous of its workings
There can be no compare
Getting an unnumbered people
From the nations everywhere

The making of a new society
The foundation of a new earth
Where unity, love and peace
Is now being given in birth

God's holy spirit is behind this
It is the source of it all
The force making all things new
It is Jehovah's beckon call

Worthy of Consideration

Do give attention all you people
To what is being foretold
Of the wayward course
Of life being lived
So immoral and so bold

A way of life that is condemned
By the one who says
This way don't live
Who knows what is best for you
Heed His call, good gifts He will give

This carrying God continues to wait
To give all a chance to live right
And turn aside from this
Wayward course and share
With Him in His delight

Please give attention you people
To what time will bring
Distressful times with
No way out foreboding
Will be these thing

Given to Disarray

I came, I saw, and after looking
At the condition of the world today
Chaotic in its appearance
And getting worse in every way

The rampaging violence of this world
Immorality arid like never before
Wars that are ever unceasing
Peace and security man cannot restore

Conditions that exceed normal bounds
And what the mind can understand
Disarrayed and out of control
Are the people throughout the land

That what this world do offer us
Can't satisfy a longing of worth
Promises made but can't be kept
In reality, what are they worth

I came, I saw, and after looking
At the condition of the world today
Chaotic in its appearance
And getting worse in every way

The House the Man

There is a house on Primrose Lane
A house that did intrigue me
It was graceful not inane
Gothic in appearance it was to me

In the shadows among the trees
In evening at the close of day
The coming of night and its breeze
Brought eerie sounds of the bay

Some say it was once occupied
By an old man who longed for days of yore
His way was odd and some did deride
Unaware of his possession in the way of lore

When time came for him to go his way
Nothing of possession did he take
Not even the sound from across the bay
Everything there was he did forsake

When he left that house on Primrose Lane
Unoccupied it stands to this day
Not so graceful yet it remains
So too the eerie sound of the bay

On the Horizon

Yonder on the far horizon
Something I did see
A movement my eyes beheld
Like waters running free

Like waters on the horizon
Glimmering in the morning sun
Over parched ground it was flowing
Like a river on the run

The movement that my eyes beheld
Were people on the march
In unison they were singing low
As they continued their march

Men and women, boys and girls
On their way to the market place
Because of the heat of the midday sun
This caused them to quicken their pace

Have you ever seen a crowd of people
Walking in the distance far away
Against the sky in the morning sun
They glimmer like water far away

Sharing Life's Problems

Life's problems are never done
Existing from days of long ago
Exemptions are not given to anyone
All are subject to the status quo

Regardless of our lot in life
Or the place where we do live
There are enough problems to suffice
If not life will freely give

Our way of life difference will show
Yet life's problems confront us all
Not passing some yet on others bestow
But make sure it effects us all

Life's problems are many and profound
One does not bear them all alone
We all are on this merry-go-round
We must face them until they are gone

Infamous

There are events that happen
Have a direct effect on us
That the flow of time may tarnish
Yet they continue with us

Events etched into our memory
Not a dream but very real
And we were part of them
This is what makes them real

The incident at Pearl Harbor
Plunged us into a world war
It changed our lives abruptly
In ways no one foresaw

We can't forget the day 9.11.01
When horror visited us by surprise
Not ready for its devastating effect
And no one to advise

Two towers basking in the sunlight
Standing firm and tall
Their hour of reckoning was near
On its arrival they would fall

These events that happen to us
Came without a sounding alarm
To wreak devastation and fear
To demoralize and do much harm

These events remind us
From the past where they live
They are not forgotten with passing time
In infamy they will live

Love's Greatest Expression

God made us in His image
To reflect His attributes
Love, power, wisdom and justice
This is what He constitutes

He is called the happy God
As the Bible says
And we can find true happiness
By walking in the light of His way

He prepared a home for man
In Eden long ago
A garden He planted Himself
The garden of God He called it so

But an event did occur one day
Instigated by an unseen source
Resulted in the loss of Paradise
Put man on a disastrous course

God knew man's hopeless condition
And He came to his rescue
Making the way for him to be redeemed
From the disobedient act of a few

Love for mankind did He prove
The greatest expression known
Love expressed beyond compare
By a Father and Son as shown

The Merry-Go-Round of Life

This merry-go-round that we are on
It is not something new
Many have ridden it before
Some of them we knew

I came on board at my birth
Like all of us did do
I have been riding its ups and downs
Since nineteen thirty-two

Many are its ups and downs
On its uncharted course
Through seas unknown it takes us
With problems from an unseen source

Life's merry-go-round and its ups and downs
On its uncharted course
Through seas unknown it yet takes us
But we now know its source

Going with the Flow of Time

My journey through the space of time
Here on earth below
Traveling with the flow of time
To a place that I don't want to go

A way of traveling that goes one way
A way of no return
A way that is filled with many problems
And I face them with deep concern

The flow of time takes me along
If I want to go or not
The flow of time I can't prolong
So its effect is my lot

My journey through the space of time
Is one I can't defer
My traveling with the flow of time
Who can I ask for a refer

No Way Out

The condition of our deteriorating state
Was made known long ago
With the passing of time the record showed
How events would become just so

The record showed how true the saying is
What is made wrong can't end right
Or that with a crook can't be made straight
Nor can our dismal plight

Like a house with a faulty foundation
Where repairs don't work at all
All you have done on it proved hopeless
It is ready for the wrecking ball

So is our distressful state
A situation with no way out
It was made wrong it can't end right
Being filled with dismay and doubt

The plight of our deteriorating state
And its inevitable downfall
Like a house with a faulty foundation
The solution is the wrecking ball

A Special Place for Me

I know a place where I can go
For an easing of the mind
No pathway is there to lead me
To this place that is hard to find

It is a place that is so unique
In making the past live again
It is a place where I often go
Yet a short time there I remain

It is a place of former times
It deals with past events
Of things that are dear to me
Yet no messages are ever sent

This place I make mention of
And why it is hard to find
I must give it complete repose
To gain the reflections of the mind

After the Lie Is Told

Once the lie the liar has told
The lie he must justify
The truth he must now distort
And the lie he must amplify

As with the first lie that was told
Involved not just the liar himself
It brought ruin to billions of others
And condemnation to himself—guilty

No liar has the intention
To promote the lie alone
Cunningly he engages others
To aid him in an undertone

He constantly upholds the lie
Speaking ever so bold
Being a master of deception
He lures others into his fold

Now a throng supports the lie
In unison they cry out aloud
How things will be if you don't comply
With the liar and his crowd

The liar and those who support his lie
For them there is no repose
The lie that was fermented and upheld
Truthfully will be exposed

Staying Close to Hope

Very often we are confronted
With things beyond our control
When situations can't be remedied
And help is limited we are told

Refusing to be a quitter
And give up what is called hope
Though the task might be bitter
Dearly, we cling to hope

While the situation may be dire
A change will come we hope
Giving not to feelings of despair
Staying ever so close to hope

We can't easily give up completely
And cast aside our feelings of hope
And walk away dejectedly
As long as there is hope

Tho' things might not get better
It won't stop our longing for hope
For a change from worse to better
What would we have if not hope

A Rampaging Malady

The madness of this world today
Goes far beyond compare
Its works and deeds are on display
Works and deeds beyond compare

Madness above all illumination
Causing the abnormal to abound
Make for worse present situations
That cause woeful cries to resound.

A madness that many do conform to
Accepting it as a way of life
The senseless things that are done
That cause many pain and strife

This madness will not correct itself
Nor can society give it a cure
It is a malady that feeds on itself
It makes all feelings insecure

This malady that abounds today
Its effect is seen in the course it takes
Mind and heart it fills with dismay
Yet a hope of relief we will partake

Let us not give up but stay the course
Against this malady that is today
Help will come from the only source
That can bring true peace in every way

A Hopeless World

The attitude of this world today
Where the norm is me me me
Is causing many to go astray
Forgetting how things should be

The callousness of ways and thought
That prevail among people today
Are living examples how some were taught
Examples that are filled with dismay

The conduct of this world as shown
Has reached an all time low
By doing bad things once unknown
That has never been done before

Not knowing the things that await us
If a change for good does not arrive
If moral breakdown remains with us
How can we as a people survive

Long Waited For

Rising early in the morning
Having waited for this day
For a journey that would take me
To the countryside far away

A country road that leads me
To a path that is seldom walked
To a woodland of greenery
Where unseen animals stalked

A meadow that lay before me
Where wild flowers' beauty is seen
The air is cool serenity abide
As hills lay bare picturesque scenes

This seldom walked path led me
To scenes of beauty that were untold
That the countryside is filled with
And many more to behold

My meandering walk continues
Along a river without end
Bring me back to the road that leads me
From the path of my journey's end

Examples That Live On

Footprints left in the sand of time
Tho' long they have been gone
Left by my mom and dad
In my mind they live on

Examples left for me to follow
Were not so easy at all
How to conduct myself in deed and words
And give due respect to all

Control your temper and tongue they said
This is what makes a wise head
Self-control of these two things
Can prolong what you might dread

Think before you speak or act
Do all you can to make peace
Humility can turn away wrath
And cause anger to cease

The examples left for me to follow
Tho' mom and dad are gone
Are a guide for me today
Etched in my mind they live on

The World's Problem Solver

I looked at the world condition
From every angle of view
The problems we are facing
Are many not just a few

On the horizon of this world
Are many problems man can't solve
And new ones are coming to birth
To test his strained resolve

These problems we are facing
What if they are not for us to solve
But are part of a greater plan
And someone else to resolve

The problems that confront us
Are found wherever man resides
From bad to worse in makeup
In every form possible worldwide

Who is this someone else
Who has the power to resolve
Who can make right what is wrong
And our many problems solve

It is the God of heaven and earth
Who knows what is best for everything
He will all our problems solve
And peace to the earth He will bring

Being Ever On Time

With the sun rising on the horizon
Giving birth to a brand new day
Many hours of stellar traveling
Arriving on time without delay

Pushing the darkness of night aside
Ready to share its light anew
Giving its rays to the earth below
Its inherent spirit it renew

Fulfilling the task it was to do
Its trek across the heavens on time
A light bearer it is for each day
Old in its origin youthful in its prime

When the sunrise on the horizon
A new day comes to view
It has kept its appointment
To share with the earth its light anew

True Friendship

How do you measure true friendship
On a scale of one to ten
Dependable and ever ready
One on whom you can depend

Always ready to lend a hand
Whenever called upon
Never hesitates or gives excuses
But offers a shoulder to lean on

No matter what the situation is
It will share an up-building thought
Acting in harmony and good of will
Sharing true feeling as one ought

True friendship can't be measured
On a scale of one to ten
It goes beyond what the scale shows
Relations that will endure to the end

A Work That Brings Joy

How different it is
To look around
And see the joy
That does abound

By a people who are
No part of this world
Yet their joy is shared
All over the world

Their joy is derived
From a work worldwide
About a coming kingdom
Where true peace will abide

This kingdom is the hope
For all mankind
By a king who will rectify
The problems of mankind

They share their joy in telling
What this kingdom will bring to birth
By the king of this kingdom
For all here on earth

At the end of a thousand year reign
His work will be recognized
The earth will then be
A worldwide Paradise
To those who have a hearing ear
To those who refuse this good news

Since this good news is to be told
Everywhere on earth
Their joy is made full as this good news
Is told in all the earth

This Long-Running Wrong

There are those who want to make
This long-running wrong right
But has found this to be
A hard and endless fight

When the wrong has been imprinted
In the heart and on the mind
This can cause many to act
In ways that are unkind

When the mind has become warped
In a distorted way
This embolds the treacherous heart
To resist in every way

And causes the mass to support
The entrenched status quo
Their hearts have become cold
And uncaring as it goes

Giving a little to appease
Don't hide this long-running wrong
Beneath its murky surface
It is still running strong

For those who support its way
Outweighs those who don't
And those who don't are the ones
Who are in need of want

This long-running-wrong society
Is much alive today
And has no intention
Of ever going away

For in the hearts of many
They want it to live on
Not having any remorse
For the wrong that is going on

This long-running-wrong society
Will soon come to its end
By the only power that does
Over everything transcends

It will change all things
And make right all that is wrong
That this long-running wrong society
Has upheld so long

A Worldwide Paradise

I freed my mind
And let it take leave
It soared beyond
This zone and time
To a world beyond
My imagination
A different world and time

As I left this known world behind
By stepping into the corridors of time
I viewed a world with true peace and security
A different world and time

A world prepared
For a certain people
A people of one accord
Who have passed the test
To reside therein
By the one whom
This world can afford

As I gaze upon what my eyes beheld
A world of endless time
A world not tainted
With satanic influences
A world that cannot decline

A world picture perfect
Painted by the master painter himself
A world that declares his perfection
Glorifying him and no one else

This world he promised is a paradise
A paradise here on the Earth
A promise he made to himself
A promise he will bring to birth

This different world is paradise
His purpose for the earth
The time is fast approaching
For this to be given in birth

Youth Be On Guard

This I can deal with and not be
Overcome by all the wrongdoing
That goes on today
But if our mental guard is ever
Let down, it only takes a moment
To lean the other way

The doing of wrong is made to look
Like it is right by those who want you
To be called one of them
They say live for today, do everything
You can, why wait for tomorrow
Do it on a whim

The counsel they give you is not
For your good disastrous it will be
If you heed its call
Acting presumptuous without giving
Any thought brings one more quickly
To a hasty downfall

You might say I can deal with anything
That may arise, I know what the limits are
And how far to go
What if things get out of hand before you
Can have a say, how will you reply to all who
Say sorry, we told you so

This is for all youth today who think
They know it all, who say times have changed
More room is what I need
To make my own decisions, forget
The teaching of old, the advice that has
In store for me, this I will not need

Who will you turn to when your time of need
Arrives and your world at that time
Comes crashing down on you
Then the wisdom of old will not benefit
You then, then you will know your unwise
Acts brought this on you

For our wrong we often say we learn
From our mistakes making it easy to put
The blame on the saying of old
None of us are perfect, all err at times
This makes it easy to say bought learned
Is better than being told

This might be true if the wrong can be
Overlooked what if it is serious enough
For justice to be served
If something can't be replaced and time
Is paramount then justice must render
A payment that is well deserved

The payment that is rendered whatever
It might be it might be hard to accept
As well as to bear
By saying the wrong that was did in it
I had no part, you being there will say
You did have a share

Those who say follow me into the doing
Of wrong, they care not about you
Or have your interest at heart
Openly they say nothing bad will
Befall you, they have opened the way
For you to have an active part

To That Which Might Look Good

Be leery of what comes your way
That look so good in its display
It can be hiding many things
And many problems this can bring

The world is master at making
The bad look like good
Its concealment and deception
Is not easily understood

To hide its flaws it has stooped
To an all time low
Deception is its way
Uncaring as it go

That what is wrong will not
Affect a well trained mind
And cause one to work
That what is unkind

The eye of the mind in discernment
Many things can behold
Things that are well hidden
Things that we are not told

The mind often tells us
When we should be aware
When something is not right
And can be a hidden snare

Give some thought before you act
To what you want or need
Later you might be glad to say
My mind I did heed

It is wise to give heed to counsel
On the saying of old
All that shines and glitters
Is not made of gold

Things that are used to snare us
Is not something new
Their hidden design are the same
Only in a different view

What Is This World Coming To?

Have you ever asked yourself
What is this world coming to?
People are doing anything
That they want to

There is no sense of remorse
Whatever they do is right
Moral values are at their lowest
Point resist and you must fight

What was once looked upon
As being morally wrong
Are being accepted openly
And are ever growing strong

There is no more hiding
The closet door is open wide
Resistance is eroding making it
Hard to stem the tide

Moral law that was set
By the highest power known
Are being opposed by many
As it is openly shown

Sure as the saying of old is
You will reap what you sow
The deeds they are now working
One day will bring them low

The day will come for them to reap
The fruitage of their toil
The end result for them will be
The reward of their toil

The seed they are sowing now
One day they will reap
When that time does arrive
They will have to weep

Failing to heed the moral law
That came direct from God
Who never changes so they must
Answer direct to God

God made man and woman and
Married them husband and wife
Not man and man nor woman and woman
And joined them for life

The union was made for them
To bring new life to birth
For he said to them become many
And fill the earth

This mandate to man and woman
He helped them to fulfill
No other way would he bless
It was his expressed will

No other way would he bless
For what he wanted them to do
This prompts me and others to ask
What is this world coming to?

In My Solitude

Many times it often happens
When I am all alone
My mind does go wandering
On its very own

Being by myself in a pensive mood
It is easy for me
to be overcome
In my solitude

Many places my mind in wandering
Does often revisit
Free as it travels
Having nothing to forfeit

The memories of its journey
Fit a special brood
As it carefully takes me along
In my solitude

Recalling many things
As it takes me along
Events I well remember
Sometimes a song

Places I have been to
People I once knew
Some things I can't recall
And names just a few

My mind is my companion
I give it due respect
On many things and in many ways
It helps me to reflect

On memories that are precious
That fit a special brood
Of things that once were live again with me
In my solitude

Memories of Kathelene

How well I do remember
A car that I once had
That held a place in my heart
For making me feel bad

This car was dear to me
Though I didn't keep it clean
It reminded me of a lady friend
So I named it Kathelene

At times it could be onery
And stubborn as a mule
Which made me feel that it was
Worthy of my ridicule

At the onset of our journey
These words I would say
Here we go again Kathe
Tell me you are going to obey

She never failed to start
This brought a smile to my face
Making me feel that Kathe
Was ready for the race

Yet knowing she might suddenly
Stop for she was mean
This would prompt me to say
Please take me home Kathelene

My patience with her was on the wane
It was time for her to go
You are so unreliable
I don't want you anymore

She looked at me as if to say
You think I am of no account
Fool, I will tell you what my problem is
A broken motor mount

With a remorseful heart I gave in
And had the problem fixed
Yet my feelings for her now
Are weak and mixed

I found out she wasn't so ornery
And not at all so mean
And she did obey me when I said
Take me home please, Kathelene

Take me home, Kathe please
Take me home, Kathelene

In Search Of

No doubt you have heard
Some talk about it
How some men have
And still strive to find it

In hope of a return
To their days of youth
By this sought for fountain
The fountain of youth

Their quest for this fountain
Is their main endeavor
They will keep searching for it
If it takes forever

Like trying to find the needle
In the mound haystack
Only to have heartbreaking effort
And many setbacks

For the enemy of youth
Is the passing of time
That takes away our youth
With the flow of time

Until time is brought
To a complete standstill
This fountain of youth
Will be elusive until

What they are seeking
They are looking the wrong way
The fountain of youth will be
A reality one day

For the one who holds time
In the palm of his hands
Assures us that one day
Youth will forever stand

Making the Impossible Possible

Being fleshly in our makeup
And origin of the dust
In life confines yet facing
Its problems that is a must

Knowing our best of effort
Will not always prevail
In view of imperfection
Prone to err we bewail

Being limited in our effort
A helper we do need
One who is in full control
A worker of impossible deeds

Since the condition that confronts us
Is grave in its scope
Looming ever darker
Void of any hope

Yet there is hope for us
From God who cannot lie
Whose purpose in himself
Our condition to rectify

The reality of his purpose
Impossible to us they seem
How and why this must be
For us to be redeemed

Here is to God above
Whom we cannot see
Who works what we call
The impossibility

For what we call impossible
To him it is unheard
If he wills for it to be
To him it has occurred

You great wondrous worker
Who causes the impossible to be
The magnitude of your greatness
Will be for all to see

No more will there be any reason
To doubt your ability
Your wondrous work will be
On display throughout eternity

The Great Pacific Ocean

You great Pacific Ocean
With boundaries wide and deep
The vastness of your waters
Are contained by decree
Within the confines of your realm
Many forms of life do creep
The form of life you contain
Is not yours you must agree

The vastness of your waters
Are wonders to behold
The depth and width that is with you
Is too profound to understand
Many things about you in times past
Have often been told
By those who have traversed you
From many different lands

To behold you in your anger
Tossed about by mighty waves
Thunderous sounds are your making
When your anger is unleashed
In the mightiness of your tempest
When everything seems unsafe
No calmness anywhere is found
Your anger is yet unleashed

The mighty wind churns about
Upsetting your watery deep
Your mighty waves uncontrolled
In anger they lash out
To upset anything that is found
Upon your watery deep
Spreading Fear and Terror
And dismay on all things round about

You great Pacific Ocean
After your waters have been made still
Your angry waves have been calmed
Roll gentle on your watery deep
Within the confine of your realm
Now lie a time of Tranquil
For once again a smile has come
To the face of your watery deep

Running for Life

This race for life that I run
It has always called for speed
Its course is broad and enticing
With many wrong signs to read

Young and with lots of time I thought
Carefree and in my prime
Having no time for important things
Nor the signs of the fleeting time

The years are many I thought
Time did not matter at all
The years were slowly passing by
As I ignored their warning call

This race for life means much more
Than this life that is known
This life that is temporary
As this life has always shown

It is life in a fuller meaning
For death will be no more
Life will be as it was meant to be
Forever Forever Forever more

My race for life in this aspect
Has prompted me even more
To run this race as valiantly
Like I have never run before

To be stout hearted and unwavering
In my faith hope and trust
On the promise of Him the Amen
The one I know I can trust

This race for life I have not won
The things of this world I cannot carry
To be victorious in this enduring race
This is not the time for me to tarry

Har-ma-ged' on

A word of fear for many today
Because they don't understand
Fear based on what man can do
With what he has at hand

Fear of destroying earth and life
Bringing Harmagedon to birth
Not knowing what Harmagedon is
And what it will bring to birth

Just what is Harmagedon
Not what many people think it to be
Something brought about by man
According to his ability

It is a war that is yet to come
A war that will end all wars
A war selective in its makeup
Harmagedon is this war

It is the war of God Almighty
A cleansing work it will perform
Ridding the earth of entrenched evil
By a global cleansing storm

Since it is global war
It will be fought everywhere on earth
Against the forces of all evil
Removing all evil from the earth

It is God's righteous war
Against the ungodly everywhere
By a commander with a sure promise
True Peace and security everywhere

Harmagedon will end something old
A wicked system that must go
Giving birth to a new order of things
And paradise forever more

Edd's Last Hoorah

O what a grand occasion
We shared in yesterday
Brothers and sisters came together
With love on display

Something that is seldom seen
Or practiced by Satan's world
Love based on Godly principal
Love that is unfurled

A token of what is yet to come
By God and to His fame
To fill the earth end to end
With a people of His name

Who will live in harmony
With His creative plan
A glimpse of this was shown
By his unseen hand

An unseen hand that can do
What He wants to be
Fulfilling His stated will
Who said this will be

Unfailing in His purpose
Was manifest this day
As people of different races
Showed love in a godly way

But this was not the beginning
It is shown in a greater way
At conventions and assemblies
That are widely held today

Where many people earth wide
Gather to show their worth
With the working of God's spirit
He is bringing this to birth

This occasion was Edd's last hoorah
We thank you for letting us
Share this with you
A moment we will cherish
In memory of you
For bringing friends together
Was so thoughtful of you

The Folly of Man

O foolish man can't you see
What you are working cannot be
You look at things
From a fleshly way
That is why things are
As they are today

What you are promoting
Is what you initiated
You failed to heed Jehovah, who created
Who said the Earth I give to the sons of men
Never said the heavenly planets
They would one day win

You are ruining things here
On the Earth below
To the planets of the heavens
Now you want to go
God did not create these
For a fleshly way of life
That promotes enmity and rivalry
Discord and strife.

In your limited knowledge
Your effort will be in vain
The foolishness of your proud wisdom
Will not let you attain
What you are in quest of
It is not for you to claim
No matter what your profound endeavor is
To make this your aim

You have failed to take care
Of the Earth here below
O how you have messed up
Everywhere your footsteps go
You do not heed what God says
He will bring to birth
That is to bring to ruin those
Who are ruining the Earth

To Unsolved Problems

As the hands on the clock
On its journey goes around
Through the hours of the day
As they near their end
When the activity of the day
Began to slow down
Soon a time of repose
Is the message that it sends

With the endings of old hours
All problems are put on hold
To wait the arrival
Of the coming day
And greet it out rightly
With past problems of old
Starting the new day
In a frustrated way

The day begins not quiet
But in an undertone
Its problems are compounded
And remain the same
With the changing of the hours
The problems are not gone
The new hours have to deal with
This unending game

At day end when its hours
Are coming to a close
A new day of hours
Are waiting to begin
Knowing the left over problem
It rightly can't dispose
It must confront them all
As its new day begins

At the end of the day
If its problems could be solved
It would give the new day
A clean and easier start
Making the day's activity
Easier for all involved
Who would eagerly wait the new day
To have an active part

Enter My Shadow

The sky above arrayed in blue
Being crystal clear
The wind is calm its stillness says
It is at rest
The sun is shining everywhere
Its warmth is a glow
A feeling of tranquil does abound
With a formal zest

Here on earth below dressed
In colors many
Blue, yellow, red and white, brown
As well as green
These are some that I mention
Yet many more exist
In places were the eye can't see
Many remain unseen

On a bright sunny day when I think
I am all alone
Only to find I have a companion
Who does exactly as I do
Every turn and footstep that I make
Every gesture as well
He duplicates my every move
As good as I can do

My companion is my shadow that the
Sunlight brings to view
Void of eyes to see
Yet he is never unaware
Being ever so nimble in movement
In copying my every move
I marvel at his style of me
I relish in his fanfare

Those We Contend With

When you wake up in the morning
After a night of much needed rest
From a previous day of harassment
From all kinds of idiots doing
What they do best

There are the idiots who walk along
Eating as they go their way
Caring not about the neighborhood
Leaving their garbage on
Public display

There are the idiots who are filthy
Of mouth odious and vulgar, they are
Being narrow of mind
Filled with hateful pride from these
You want to keep afar

There are the idiots who have no code
Of dress loose and baggy like clowns
If you don't copy
Their dress and style
You are looked upon with a hateful frown

Here is to the idiots of idiots who drive the
Automobile who think they set
The standards of the road
On how we should act when
Behind the steering wheel

These are the most dangerous idiots of idiots
In jeopardizing many lives
They vent their displeasure
In a fit of rage in their
Love of violence they do thrive

These that I make mention of we
Contend with them each day
We are glad for a night of freedom
From them yet our foe they
Will be with the coming day

The idiots that I have characterized here
Pertain to all who are rude and bold
Both men and women can be idiots if they
Both correctly fit the mold

The Folly of Evolution

The theory of evolution
No way has it been proved true
Nor what so-called wise ones say
No way can it be true

Who believes that life evolved
In ways it could not
And progressed through the ages
To what is now our lot

They fail to give heed
To a far superior mind
Who said things would produce
According to its kind

This he foretold
In days of long ago
And everything has produced
Just as he said so

All things have remained the same
From days of long ago
Humans and animals have produced
As he did say so

Time has not brought a change
That evolution say
Things are the same no change has come
In any way

The lower forms of life today
Are just as they were then
The animal kingdom is the same
As it has always been

When God made man in his image
Something new he did do
He brought forth a form of life
That resulted in me and you

No process of evolution
Was in God's creative plan
Therefore things would proceed
According to his plan

This leaves no room for conjecture
What evolution is based upon
There is room only for the truth
What God's word is based upon

This System Is a Rat Race

This system that we have today
It is an elusive dream
It is for those who have the means
To enjoy the best things it seems

A system upheld by the wealthy
A middle class follows behind
Then comes the poor that have not
Who are not of their kind

The rich class keeps getting richer
The middle class tries to compete
The poor keep getting poorer
For this rat race is not complete

This rat race is a treadmill
That the rich don't have to walk
An uphill walk for the middle class
While the poor laborers balk

The rich go on getting richer
The middle class tires to compete
The poor have-nots look on in vain
This rat race is not yet complete

The rich set the tone for this dream
The middle class tries to compete
The poor will not have a share
In a dream they can't compete

The rich do not share their wealth
So the middle class must compete
The poor can't contend with them
In a race where they can't compete

The poor make the rich class richer
The middle class follows suit
The poor keep getting poorer
Having no chance to follow their suit

So the rich keep getting richer
The middle class tries to compete
The poor sadly look on in vain
This rat race is not yet compete

Once there is no more rich class
Or middle class to compete
Or poor ones who look in vain
Then this rat race will be complete

To Rebecca My Wife

My darling my dear Rebecca
The flower of my dream
How well do I remember
The night when we first met
Memories to me so dear
As if yesterday they seem
Across the room from where I stood
Is the place where you sat

The relation that was formed from there
Has lasted to this day
A relation that was engraved with love
Sealed in a bond of trust
One that has endured the storms of life
Grow stronger in every way
Formed with love friendship so pure
And honesty is a must

The years we have been together
Through the uncharted course of life
Not knowing what might confront us
As we walked from day to day
As we walked together
Not as two but one in unity and love
Husband and wife
From this came the strength that helped
Us to stay on life's enduring way

In the twilight of our years
When youth has fled the scene
And fading memories of time past
So unreal they seem
The fleeting years have taken their toll
By changing many scenes
Rebecca you are still the flower
That perks me up—the flower of my dreams

Our Home the Earth

I let my eyes wander far as they
Could see
And dwell on the works of God's
Creative hand
Works that can be discerned with the
Human eye
In the heavens above and on earth
Throughout the Land

His works in the heavens show the
Skills of His hand
Many they are and in silence they
Perfectly perform
Attest to the wisdom of the
Almighty One
Within the confines of decorum
They obediently perform

He placed them afar in a realm that is
Cold and silent
An environment that is unkind to
Earthling man
Inanimate they must be to reside
Forever there in
Off limits and unlivable
For fleshly puny man

Then he made the earth for it to be
Inhabited
Forming it to his likeness with a
Purpose in view
Filling it with everything that is
Necessary for life
This would continue forever more
Being always new

Earth is the only planet made
For life completely
Unique in its makeup to sustain it
Indefinitely
No matter what man says or how far in
Space he goes
He will have to come back to the
Earth home here below

He made planet earth different from
The other ones
The only one he gave life to and
Life sustaining need
The jewel of his creation, a beautiful
Gem in space
Attesting to God's wisdom, fulfilling its
Inhabitants' needs

Keep on Waiting

It has been much talked about
From days of long ago
And all this talking about it
Has kept the fire aglow

This talking is so needed
Our faith it does whet
For it has been a long time coming
And it ain't got here yet

The promises it has in store for us
Are worth our waiting on
For they are coming from the one
Whom we can rely upon

The things that are with us today
Are not part of his plan
What we have been waiting for so long
Will complete his plan

The kingdom of God is what we have
Been waiting for so long
The only thing that can make right
All that has gone wrong

And bring all things back to the state
That he had in view
And this he said I will do
I am making all things new

We might feel like we have waited
Longer than we think
But to him who is of endless time
It is like the eye with a blink

What if we have waited a long time for it
And it ain't got here yet
Don't give up, wait on I plead
It is a wait you will not regret

So let us stand firm and wait
No matter how long it take
That which we have been waiting for
Let us wait on for heaven sake

And not be disappointed
Because it ain't got here yet
We have God's word that his kingdom
Will come on this we can bet

A Deadly Root of Evil

Money money money
It has power worldwide
It is used to feed violence
In its growing tide

When used for humane effort
Nothing is wrong with that
But if the effort becomes evil
There is a wrong with that

There are some things as we know
That money cannot buy
Things that lie beyond its power
Tho' hard you may try

Many things you need might come
From an adversary
If you don't satisfy his delight
Your need won't be temporary

Some might use what they sell
To gain a fiendish end
All the time letting you know
They are not a lasting friend

Selling their wares for your money
Planning for your demise
Helping those who will visit you
With a deadly surprise

Hate and money together
Can ferment a deadly game
To destroy a way of life
As well as to maim

Causing much destruction
Amid dismay and horror
It is the game known today
That is called terror

Many believe that money is
King of everything
And can solve the problems
That is often brings

It cannot buy friendship
Not peace of mind
Or rectify the problems
That are plaguing mankind

It can't buy love or health
Happiness it can't assure
Nor can it provide peace and security
That will forever endure

Some who accept your money
Might disagree with your will
After getting your money
They may hate you even still

The world today is motivated
By money and greed
Those who have money say
Stick with me, I will fill your need

Promising you everything
If you are loyal to their call
Help them retain the status quo
Will be a benefit to all

After the Storm

When the sky turns black
Because of the clouds
Foreboding this can be
A warning sign
In darkness enshroud
A sign for all to see

Wind once still
Now growing in strength
And moves things about
Lightning flashes at great lengths
And thunderous sound does shout

The darkening sky calls
For the raging storm
Causing all things to be in fear
Of the power that exists
Without any form
And the roaring wind
Is all that you hear

When the thunder booms
It shakes the earth
And lightning lights up the sky
The clouds are waiting to give birth
To the rain that is held high

The storm has passed
The thunder is quiet
The clouds left over are few
The wind is calm cooling but quiet
The sun reigns high in full view

The lightning has returned
To its own place
The thunder waits to be called again
The wind blows light at its own pace
The storm lies unbuilt
To be formed once again

The Beginning

I stepped into the corridor
Of Time
And found myself in the indefinite
Time Past
When darkness and water covered
Earth Worldwide
For light or life had not
Been Cast

A period when time was not a factor
In His Plan
When God's creative work began
To Appear
The bringing forth of light when He
Said for it to be
To this he said, night and day
Is Here

He divided the watery deep with
An Expanse
The expanse he called heaven that was
Above the Waters
Seas he made below the expanse for
The Earth to Appear
Preparing it for the greenery whose face
It would alter

These and other events came about as
Jehovah God Desired
Still time was not a factor in His
Creative Plan
For He existed from the indefinite
Time Past
Therefore he controlled time to use as
He Demanded

Last He said to his master worker, Let us
Make Man
In this event no allotment for time
Was Made
Time for man would be endless if God he
Would Obey
For Jehovah God in His image man
He Made

We Will Not Forget Katrina

Just when we had thought
We had overcome
The horror that had visited us on 9/11/01
Now to be visited by something
More devastating
A storm called Katrina and her evil run

The eye of the storm had formed
Not just overweight
Getting itself together
To wreak horror and much fright

The clarion call was given
To all with a hearing ear
Of the danger that was coming
Soon it would be near

As storm clouds formed on the horizon
Many did not heed the call
Taking light the looming danger
That would soon befall them all

The love of material possessions
Or not having a way out at all
Many decided
To wait out the danger
That would befall them all

With roaring wind and water
Devastation came ashore
In one place after another
Like nothing ever seen before

The fury of its power
Caused many to say so
That her destructive effect
Would be seen forever more

It came ashore in Florida
Not with the fury foretold
En route to Gulf Port, Mississippi
Where its fury would unfold

Then it ran to Biloxi
And vented its passion there
With its eye on Mobile
Her people were aware

But the power of her fury
She was saving for another place
The shores of Louisiana
New Orleans and her grace

As if it knew her levees
Would not support her weight
Heavily it leaned upon
New Orleans with all its weight

The power of her wind
Enraged and uncontrollable
The storm surge of her waters
Came with fury untold

When her flood waters began to rise
And flow everywhere
Those who did not leave
Felt their demise was there

In the dark hours of their plight
There is water everywhere
Scenes that seem so unreal unlike
The one that had existed there

Thousands had nowhere to go
And no one seems to care
As if lost in time in a different world
Without any fanfare

Katrina vented her rage
Then she moved on
But her after effect
Is yet going on

Many lives she left uncertain
In the aftermath of her wake
Consternation, pain and heartache
They will forever partake

Katrina Katrina Katrina you
And your evil run are gone
Yet memories of your ruin
In infamy will live on

No way will our mind
Ever lose sight of you
You made yourself part of us
So we must live with you

Solving the Mystery

This is for you O jack-o'-lantern
A face on the pumpkin you be
Or is there more to your identity
That we have not come to see

Referring to the dictionary
A word about you it gives us
That you are a misleading thing
A word called Ig'-nis • Fat'-u-u-s
Here is a jack-o'-lantern
Who grins from ear to ear
Whose beaming eyes are roving
Both far and near

His grin is not pleasant to look at
Being sinister in its makeup
Clearly concealing your purpose
From all who drink of your cup

Deceit is his ongoing
Causing many to become his prey
Fulfilling his evil intention to
Snaring all whom he they obey

You first made known your deception
In Eden long ago
Cunningly seducing the first woman
Saying the truth you must know

The beginning of ruination
His aim remains the same
To mislead as many as he can
By deceit and false claim

Who is this jack-o'-lantern
Whose grin manifests all evil
A grin that shows his unseen intent
He is none other than Satan, the Devil

After Katrina What?

First Katrina came and laid waste
Some of America's gulf coast
The devastation she left behind
Unbelievable it was to her host

After completing a journey of ruin
That left many in a state of woe
Disrupting and changing many lives
Made her an evil and unfriendly foe

Meantime something else was looming
In the wake of Katrina's stint
A storm named Rita was forming
With mayhem being her intent

In time she did grow in size
Slowly she began to move about
Taking her time to form an eye
To make her intention known without doubt

Over the vast waters of the Atlantic
Her destructive course she did plot
As watchful men kept her in view
For what she brought would be our lot

Doing their best preparing for the worst
They waited for it to come ashore
Not the way Katrina had trod
To areas that might not be no more

Her wind at the ready she began to move
In strength and speed she did grow
Her eye on the area she had planned ahead
Caused many to guess for they didn't know

Her eye on the area she selected
She had chosen unknown with care
Not wandering aimless around
The way she knew of getting there

On time she began her evil run
An expected visit to the Florida Keys
Maybe she would bypass New Orleans
On her way from Florida's Keys

People were sitting on pins and needles
Dreading what might come ashore
Expecting the horror it might bring
To America's gulf coast once more

Once in the Gulf of Mexico
Rita became a full hurricane force
The warm waters of the gulf
Became the energy of her source

Rita visited New Orleans by wind from ashore
Against weakened levees it didn't care
Great were the waters they had to contain
The pounding of the wind some couldn't bear

Under Rita's pounding wind
Some levees began to fail
Some of her water would overcome
When weakened levees began to fail

The object of her fury wasn't New Orleans
This she withheld for more than one place
On to Lake Charles to vent her rage there
Moving ever slowly at a leisurely pace

On to Texas with her eye on Port Arthur
But not with the power that Katrina had
Her destructive run did leave its mark
Wind and water left many feeling bad

She went to Beaumont, an uninvited guest
Her visit there they didn't want to see
For her work would not be good at all
Devastation it would be for all to see

Rita wasn't the storm many feared it to be
Her run fell short of Katrina's stint
She did not fill Katrina's large shoes
Therefore she did not repeat her stint

Memories Good and Bad

Fond memories of my life
At times I do recall
Memories that are etched
In the corridors of my mind
Memories not forgotten waiting
For the clarion call
To travel once again
The corridors of my mind

Cherished memories that are framed
In picture forms appear
Have been preserved so crystal clear
For a future time
And when they are called upon
On time they do draw near
To fill the mind once again
Of a former time

Yet there are other memories
Not so fond to be recalled
And these are also etched
In the corridors of my mind
Memories of hurtful things
Horror gone appall
A revisit by bad memories
Due to orders of its kind

Memories good and bad
The mind is fully aware
Being able to recall them
From the corridors of the mind
Being in control of events
It is never unaware
Of the flow of events it calls up
According to its kind

Memories that reside with me
Good and bad they are
Help keep my mind alert
And not become blank
The good ones I cherish
The bad ones I keep afar
To him who provides memory for me
To him do I give thanks

Both Sides of the Mirror

I stepped into the mirror to get
A view from the other side
What mine eyes beheld made me
Tremble with much fear inside

I saw a world full of strife and in turmoil
As well as being rife in moral decay
And its raging violence uncontrolled
This is the order of its present way

I saw a world full of unrest and hate
Mandated by division rooted in
Unending pride
This gives birth to opposition as well as
Restlessness that causes there to exist
A worldwide great divide

I saw a world that is without any hope
Unable to solve its problems
That grow by leaps and bounds
The wisdom of its wise ones is of no help
Like blind ones they just
Mope and grope around

Both sides of the mirror paint a picture
That is bleak; what this world needs
Must come from another source
For this world was not made
For this what is now must be brought back
To its rightful course

God's Righteous Standards

The righteous standards of God
Are not beyond our reach
He wants us to learn of them
So to us he teaches

His word the Bible enlightens us
Of his righteous ways
This makes known why it is good
To heed what it says

If we learn and uphold them
In the light of his way we tread
The way of pleasantness it is called
Freed of darkness and its dread

His standards are a safeguard
Against all fleshly desires
That we alone might succumb to
By yielding to its alluring cries

Those lofty standards are pushed aside
By most of this world today
Resulting in a moral decline
And decadent rules hold sway

For our way to be successful now
And reap the prize of the reward
We must uphold his righteous standards
To reap the promised large reward

In Lieu of the Evidence

How do you visualize something
Or someone you can't see
That is void of any shape or form
How can they possibly be

One must rely upon the mind
And form a mental picture there
Or look at the world around you
And hope to find the answer
Somewhere

Let us refer back to the mind
And what it can comprehend
As it works hard to put a face on
A shapeless personality
It must defend

Or we can look
At the world around us
And all the things that we can see
In this vast array of evidence
An intelligent form comes to be

While we can't visualize some things
Or someone we can't see
There evidence is there
That gives support
To an unseeing being
Will you agree

Sequel to Katrina and Rita 2005

First Katrina came and left
Ruin in her wake
On a scale unprecedented
On the area she did shake

After her run was over
What she left is with us today
Changed scenes, altered lives
Frustration and dismay

Katrina was the beginning
Now something else did appear
A storm named Rita was forming
At Katrina's rear

Rita made her debut
Similar to Katrina's stint
New places she did visit
Not the way Katrina went

Where she went on her run
Caused bewilderment and concern
Being an uninvited guest
Her intention people did discern

That she had a hand to play
Before she would move on
To leave many in a state of shock
Then she would be gone

With Rita gone these trying times
Hopeful they were done
But on yon horizon
There be another one

Small in its beginning now
Rapidly did it grow
This storm they named Wilma
We all would come to know

Wilma started out up and down
The wind gauge scale
This had many to believe that
Her power might not prevail

Her wind at times would lessen
Yet her direction did not change
Regardless of her movement
She stayed in hurricane range

It left the Yucatan Peninsula
Its eye on Florida's Gulf Coast
Growing in size and speed
Made her an unwanted host

What she had planned for her guest
Unwelcome it would be
Destructive wind, surging waters
Calamity was her decree

It came across Florida's peninsula
Weakened to some degree
She had the power to wreak havoc
That many eyes would see

Moving swiftly on her journey
She was thanked for doing this
For a quick departure of her visit
Many places she would miss

Katrina and Rita, Wilma to Will
Became part of the past
Yet memories of them with us
A long time they will last

May time allow us for a while
Not to be visited by another one
They we might heal but not forget
Them and their evil run

These that I make mention of
Are not the only one
Others have visited us this year
Less vicious on their run

All are compiled in the data
The storms of 2005
The ruin, the changing of many scenes
And altering many lives

The hurricane season is not over
It still resides with us
We wait for other that may come
Living in fear and disgust

All of us are affected by them
Either directly or not
Their often presence tells us
This will be our lot

There or Here

There is a controversy
With you and me
On a subject that we both
Never do agree

When we are not together
Either far or near
If I ask you, are you there
You say I am here

When I ask you politely
How can this be
For presently
You are not here with me

Finally you retort and say
You know you are there
What is left for me to say
But I know that I am here

We have our ups and downs
About where we are
It doesn't matter to us
If we are near or far

The question was a way
In our talking to appear
It always came to this
Are you there or am I here

This controversy continues
Without an end in sight
Both of us contend
That each is in the right

For the place that I am in
To you it is there
It really doesn't matter
As long as I am here

Maybe there is no answer
To what we are asking here
When I ask you are you there
To you, you are here

If to you, you are here
Then to you, I am there
For here to you is there
Yet there to me is not here

The End of Death

O enemy Death
Be not ever so proud
That your reign has caused much
Sorrow and weeping aloud

In the heart of many
You have instilled much fear
But now, O Death
Your reign and end is near

You have reigned as king
From days of long ago
Installed by one man who
Couldn't say he didn't know

Your trek throughout the earth
Relentless it has been
A journey that seems to be
One without end

Throughout the earth you
Have visited everywhere
Watching your subjects that
Are ever present there

Knowing they are subjects
Of your domain
Come what may eventually
Those you will claim

O Death, how you have stalked us
Being ever so proud
That your reign has caused much
Agony and crying aloud

Soon we will not be subjects
Of your domain
Soon you will not have the power
Over us to reclaim

For God has set the time
For your reign to end
For over you, O Death
He does transcend

He will take away the power
That you had before
Bringing you to nothing
Then you will be no more